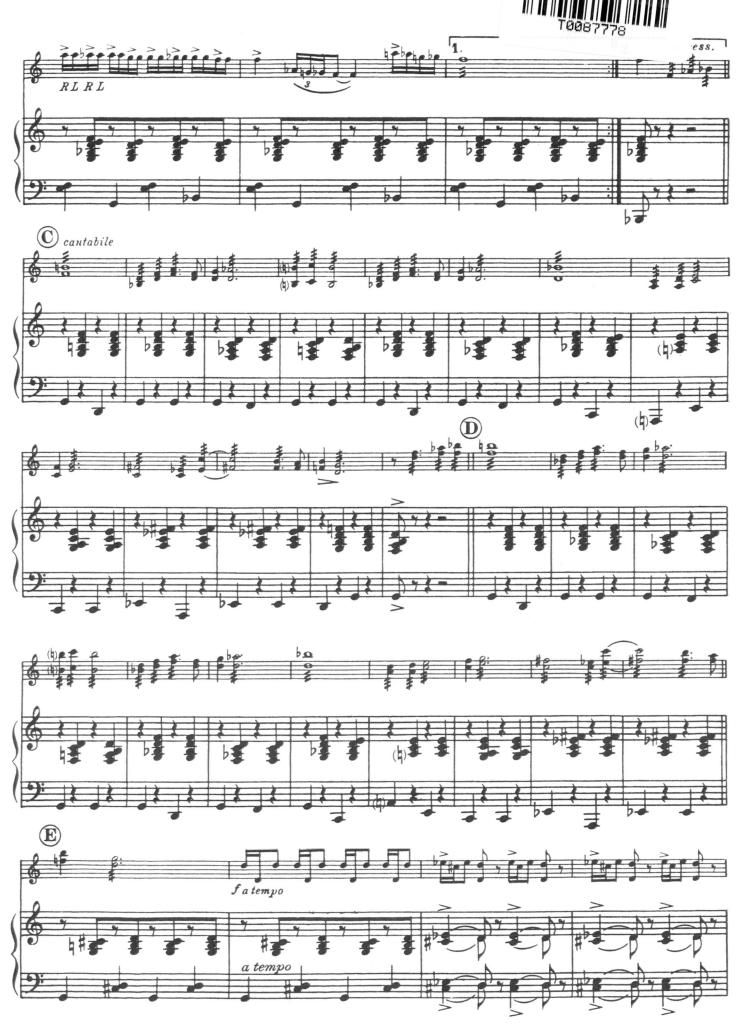

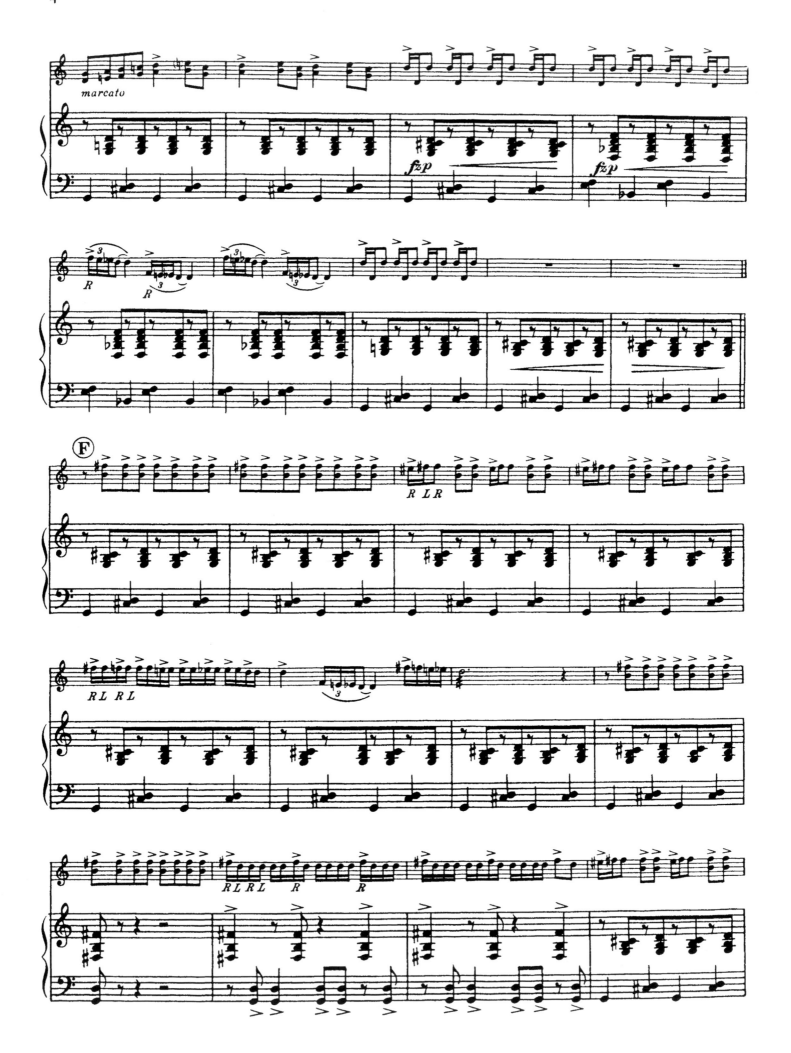

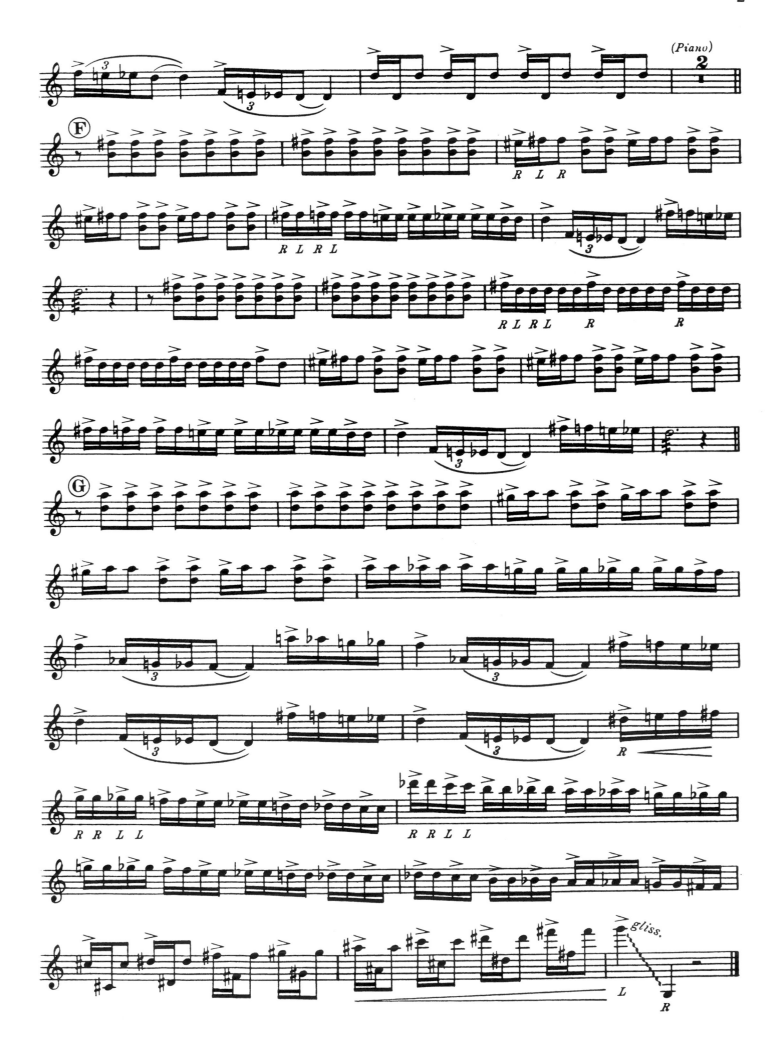

SABRE DANCE
from "GAYANE BALLET"

Xylophone Solo

Aram Khachaturian
Arranged for Xylophone and Piano by
Morris Goldenberg

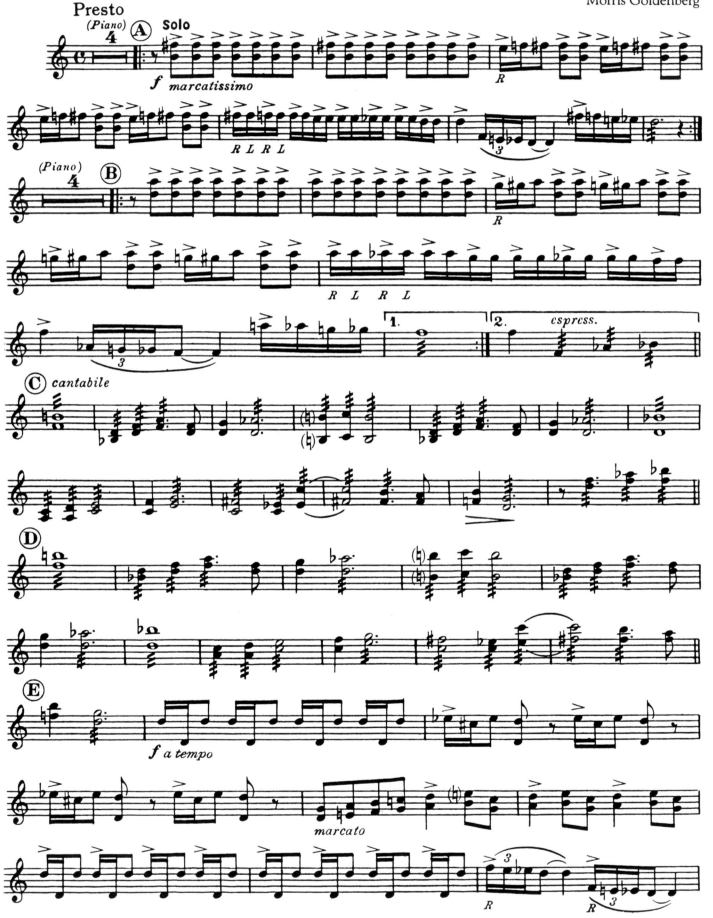

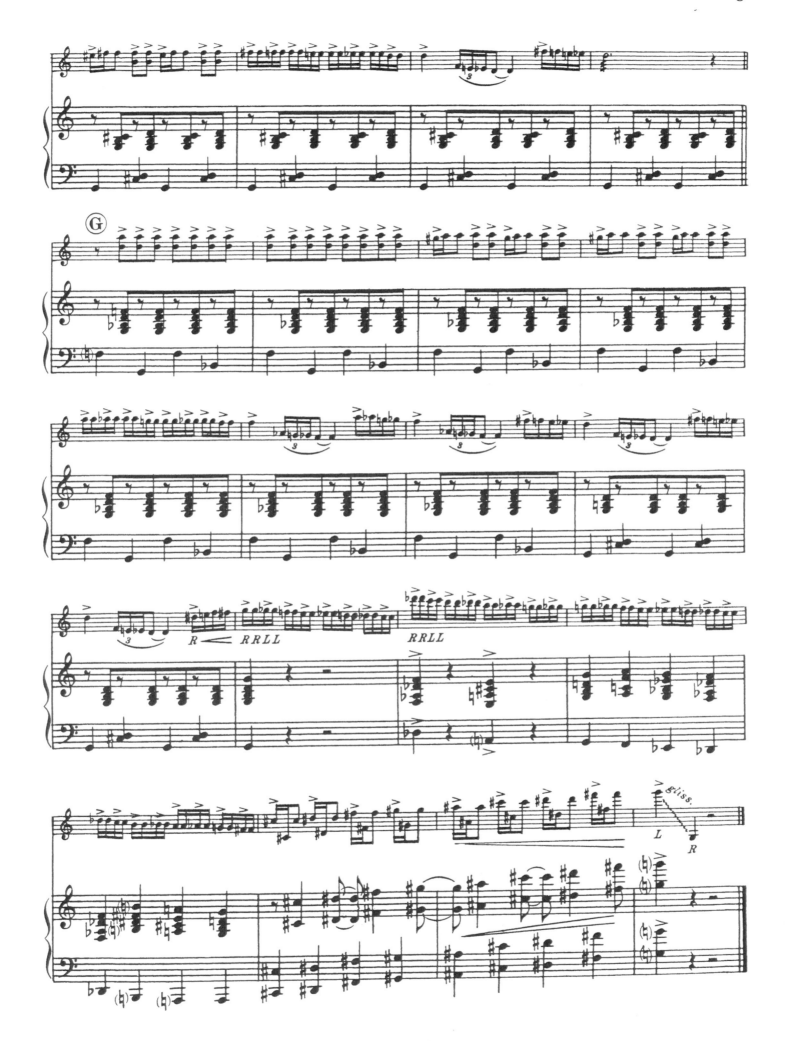

U.S. $7.99

8 84088 49615 9

HL50490096

ISBN 978-1-4234-7756-3

9 781423 477563